MODERN IDOLATRY AND THE END OF THE WORLD

AVRAHAM GILEADI

HEBRAEUS PRESS

Modern Idolatry and the End of the World
© Copyright 2018 by Hebraeus Press
www.IsaiahInstitute.com
All rights reserved
Published in the United States of America
First printing, 2017
Softcover ISBN 978-0-910511-41-4
E-Book ISBN 978-0-910511-42-1

CONTENTS

PREFACE

Because the most reliable endtime guide next to direct prophecy consists of scriptural *types* or *patterns* from the past, Israel's prophets in large part prophesy using such types as foreshadowings of the future. Parallels between ancient Israel and spiritual Israel today, for example, provide a yardstick for how we measure up with God's people in the past. In that way, they inform us of what we may expect to happen in the imminent future.

1

Defining Idolatry

When speaking of idolatry, we may be tempted to think of people venerating statues, bowing down before "dumb idols," or participating in processions with icons raised on portable pedestals. While today some religious communities perpetuate these ancient kinds of worship, idol worship assumes many forms besides these, less tangible perhaps than statue worship but just as virulent.

In essence, idolatry comprises any activity that diverts a worshiper's attention from the true God and his law to a counterfeit. The first of the Ten Commandments warns against worshiping false gods: "You shall have no other gods before me" (Deuteronomy 5:7). The commandment then depicts idolatry as anything less than loving "Jehovah your God with all your heart, with all your soul, and with all your might" (Deuteronomy 6:5). Israel's earliest history is full of admonitions to refrain from "going after the gods of the peoples round about" (Deuteronomy 6:14; cf. Joshua 23:6–8).

Those ground rules let everyone know that true worship exists within a *narrow* compass. Idolatry, on the other hand, takes the *broad* way—the way of the world and the Gentile nations surrounding Israel. God's people maintained their special covenant status so long as they worshiped God alone, not the gods of the nations (Deuteronomy 7:1–11; Isaiah 50:1; Hosea 1:2–9).

As Israel's conquest of the Land of Canaan shows, God ultimately destroys and dispossesses people who indulge in idol worship (Deuteronomy 28:15–68; Isaiah 65:1–7, 11–15; Jeremiah 44:2–14). And yet, even in the face of God's performing amazing miracles for ancient Israel, his people jeopardized their chosen status by adopting the way of the Gentiles. When they didn't repent of the idolatrous practices they learned from the Gentile nations, God cut the Israelites off from his presence and many perished. In another instance of idolatry, he removed the gospel from one group of people and gave it to another (Romans 11:11).

In only few and special circumstances was idolatry indeed entirely absent from any people of God. Our concern, therefore, shouldn't center on the fact that many people today knowingly or unknowingly practice idolatry. What poses a concern is idolatry's becoming so widespread that it affects all. God's condemnation of his people occurs when offenders among them become the majority.

The reality is that the worldly practices that are enticing so many people have the power to deceive the heart (Deuteronomy 11:16). The whole *heart* must be occupied with the things of God, must constantly "remember" his commandments in order to maintain true worship (Numbers 15:39–41). When the hearts of God's people are "changed" by their idolatries, they grow alienated from God so that they can't hear with their spiritual ears (Deuteronomy 30:17).

Because idolatry is an inductive practice, once people get caught up in it, the habit carries its own momentum and supplies its own rationale. God gave Israel a special charge, therefore, never to depart from his commandments either "to the right hand or to the left" (Deuteronomy 5:32). When observing these commandments, Israel was told not to add to or diminish from them (Deuteronomy 12:32). The worship of God must not merely encompass the whole heart but must retain its purity as well. True worship leaves no aspect of life unaccounted for by divine law. Israel's righteousness has ever been synonymous with observing to "do all these commandments before Jehovah our God as he has commanded" (Deuteronomy 6:25).

2

COEXISTENCE OF TRUE AND FALSE WORSHIP

In pointing out parallels of idolatry between God's people anciently and today, we mustn't presume that people worship only false gods. Worship of the true God is rarely done away. Rather, people often worship the true God alongside the false gods. They maintain a careful equilibrium in order to preserve an identity with the God of Israel, the God of their fathers, but at the same time they follow their own gods as they please. Such a compromise enables them to satisfy both their carnal instincts and their spiritual aspirations. It causes God's prophets to cry out in anguish, "Choose you this day whom you will serve" (Joshua 24:15) and "How long will you halt between two opinions?" (1 Kings 18:21).

In some instances of idolatry, worship of the true God and false gods becomes fused. Then the concept of the true God gets distorted while the false gods assume the authenticity and endorsement that belongs to the true God. Of all idolatry, God finds such syncretism most intolerable. It epitomizes the idea of "philosophies of men mingled with scripture." Things incongruent with true worship thereby acquire an aura of sanctity. For God's people, syncretism lies but one step away from severing their spiritual roots. It forms the final stage of apostasy before God brings on his judgment.

Ironically, appearances of true worship persist in every stage of apostasy. Laying stress on outward observances is often a symptom of alienation from the true God. When false gods are the order of the day, people feel the need to scrupulously preserve the exterior of true worship. People who reach that point confuse righteousness with actively congregating and religiously performing ecclesiastical duties. In such worship, institutional conventions can become the enemy of spontaneity, resulting in dead, stereotypical devotion.

The writings of Isaiah, pertinent to our day, commence with his indictment of those who actively attend religious meetings, who multiply sacrifices at the temple (Isaiah 1:11–14; cf. Jeremiah 7:1–15). In actuality, the people of Jerusalem had "changed their gods" (Jeremiah 2:11). Their land was desolated because they were committing abominations, "whoring after their idols" (Ezekiel 6:9).

Anciently, idol worship preceded divine judgments such as cataclysms, plagues, famine, war, destitution, and desolation. In the endtime, therefore, when all biblical types repeat themselves, we may expect "the great and dreadful day of Jehovah"—a time of God's judgment on all nations—to start when these ancient forms of idolatry reappear among his people. No scriptural type or precedent speaks of God's bringing on a universal judgment until his people who acknowledge him as their God sink into apostasy. The righteousness of the righteous can stay his judgments from the earth for a time, but the wickedness of the wicked becomes the catalyst of his judgments when the balance tips in favor of wickedness.

That pattern was established in two instances of biblical history. First, when the ten northern tribes of Israel apostatized that led to Assyria's conquest and desolation of the ancient world. And second, when the Jews of Israel's southern kingdom apostatized and Babylon repeated Assyria's scenario of destruction and exile. The prophets link both events to Israel's idolatry (Isaiah 10:3–11; Jeremiah 25:3–11; Hosea 11:1–7). By comparing wicked

Israel to Sodom and Gomorrah (Isaiah 1:10; Jeremiah 23:14; Ezekiel 16:49), the prophets allude to both Israel's fate and a deficit of righteous people (cf. Genesis 18:23–32; 19:24–29).

A story is told of a man who tried to reverse his priorities. As a young man, he wanted to have an impact on the whole world. In middle age, he wanted at least to influence his community. In his old age, he would have been glad to have converted his own family. Lastly, on his deathbed, he wished he had just improved himself. As many people have learned, God's judgments follow when people break his commandments. One individual's obedience can nevertheless bring an incalculable good. By discussing the twelve forms of idolatry that follow, I don't mean to limit things to them. Other forms of idol worship exist, but I point to these as some of the more obvious or serious.

3

WORSHIPING IMAGES

As noted, the first of the Ten Commandments prohibits God's people from having "other gods before me" (Exodus 20:3). The expression "before me" (*'al panai*), however, literally means "before my face" or "in my presence." It signifies that idolatry cuts us off from the presence of God or that an idolater can't behold his face.

But the first commandment also specifies a particular kind of idol worship—the making of "graven images" and "likenesses" (Exodus 20:4). The Hebrew words for these terms (*pesel*; *temûnâ*) possess the additional connotations of "statue" and "picture." Israel must not make for itself graven images or statues, nor make likenesses or pictures of anything in the heavens above or on the earth beneath, or in the waters below the earth (Exodus 20:4). Moses defines the scope of the prohibited imagery as "any figure . . . male or female," including the likeness of any beast, bird, reptile, or fish (Deuteronomy 4:16–18).

The purpose of this prohibition was not to inhibit the creation or enjoyment of art but to ensure that no one's heart "turn away" from God to the images (Deuteronomy 29:18)—that God's people ought not to "bend down" to them nor "serve" them (Exodus 20:5; 23:24). A strong suggestion here is that they could become a huge distraction if people began focusing on things created instead of on the Creator.

Despite the amazing miracles of deliverance Israel's God wrought for his people, they nevertheless quickly turned to other gods. The Old Testament is full of examples of their making images for themselves after they inherited the Promised Land. They made images of the god Baal and set them up in a house of Baal (1 Kings 16:32; 2 Kings 10:26–27). They set up images in their own houses (Judges 17:4; 18:30) as well as in the houses of their gods (Nahum 1:14). They made images of men and "committed whoredoms" with them (Ezekiel 16:17). They "doted" upon images of the elite of Babylonian society, images in color, of people in splendid attire (Ezekiel 23:14–16).

In homage, as it were, to a Urim and Thummim, Gideon made an image of an ephod (a vest-like garment worn by the high priest in ancient Israel), and "all Israel went whoring after it" (Judges 8:27). The worship of cleverly fashioned images became a way of life, preoccupying the craftsman and patron alike (Hosea 13:2).

Common to all this sort of idol worship was an infatuation with the *image* of a thing rather than its reality. Images require time, energy, and materials to conceive and to produce. After they are made, images represent men's labors, something to admire and "dote" over. Meanwhile, people get distracted from what is real. God is no longer central to their thoughts. They have taken something worthy of reverence out of context and destroyed its value by overemphasizing it.

Even should they realize their error, people must get a return on their investment. They can't simply discard the idol. Once it is made, the thing is hard to get rid of. Throughout this preoccupation, people "bend down" toward their idols by assigning them undue worth, all the while turning their hearts away from God. To this point, the word "serve" in Hebrew (*'abad*) (Exodus 20:5; 23:24) also means "work." Whatever people *work* at, spend time and resources on, that is what they *serve*.

In that sense, we could conclude that an obsession with unreality lies at the heart of idolatry. To idolaters, something tangible or corporeal, such as an image, possesses more appeal than something intangible and incorporeal. Even the Golden Calf supposedly represented God himself. Aaron called the orgy that attended the calf's dedication a "feast to Jehovah" (Exodus 32:4–5).

When we neither see God nor experience him, however, doesn't an image that represents him make him much more real to us? The image brings him down to *our* level, limits him to *our* perception of him. God becomes a concept we can easily deal with, something we can sketch, sculpt, or paint, and mass produce. By adjusting our image of God to our mortal notions of him, we manipulate him until the idea of God no longer threatens us. Moreover, now that we have created a false god, our void is filled. Our "minds" or "hearts" (*lebab*) are diverted, and before long we have moved away from the real God.

Those who separate themselves from things heavenly thus tend to "bend down" to an inordinate preoccupation with the "things" of this world. As illustrated by the modern media, they exchange the glory of the immortal God for images resembling mortal man, birds, and beasts (Romans 1:23). They "change . . . the truth of God into a lie," worshiping the creature rather than the Creator (Romans 1:25).

Severing their divine umbilical cord, such substitution inevitably leads to all kinds of lusts and wickedness (Romans 1:24, 26–32). When we deviate from God's way to the right or to the left, we render ourselves vulnerable to sin. We risk cutting ourselves off from God's saving grace. Idol worship, therefore, goes hand in hand with every kind of moral perversity (Exodus 32:6, 25; Leviticus 18:3–19:4; Numbers 25:1, 8; 1 Kings 14:23–24; 2 Kings 23:4–7; 1 Peter 4:3).

Because people's deference to images leads to these societal abominations, the images themselves *are* "abominations" (Deuteronomy 27:15; cf. 30:17; Isaiah 44:19; Ezekiel 20:7–8). Their price in silver and gold—now polluted—is also an "abomination," something to be burned with fire (Deuteronomy 7:25) or ground to powder (Exodus 32:20; 2 Kings 23:6, 16). By God's standard, even the idolaters themselves are "abominations" (Isaiah 41:24). The end result of their lifestyle is to "perish quickly from off the good land" God had given them (Joshua 23:16; cf. Deuteronomy 30:18).

Those who worship images thus participate in a grand subterfuge that endangers not only themselves but an entire people. As many biblical examples show, idolatry is contagious. Once a person or group of people gets caught up in it, others tend to follow (Judges 8:27; 17–18; 1 Kings 11:4; 12:28). Then, within a short time, almost "everyone is doing it." But the idolaters don't recognize what is happening to them. They become spiritually blind without realizing it (Jeremiah 51:17). Before they are aware, calamitous judgments are befalling them (1 Samuel 4–7; Jeremiah 10; Ezekiel 6–7).

In the end, the images to which people attributed power in shaping the course of history (Isaiah 48:5) are deemed worthless, becoming mere objects of mockery (Jeremiah 10:15). The final test of whether a god is true or false is whether he saves his people in God's Day of Judgment (Judges 10:13–14; Isaiah 37:18–20; Jeremiah 11:10–15). The ancient prophets made sport of those who, rejecting the true God, clung to false gods for deliverance in the time of trouble (Isaiah 44:9–20; 46:1–7; Jeremiah 2:28).

Meanwhile, no one expected such adverse results. Among idol worshipers no clear perception exists of impending calamity (Isaiah 57:1). Idolaters are "unaware and insensible" of God's hand in the affairs of men. "Their eyes are glazed so they cannot see, their minds are incapable of discernment" (Isaiah 44:18). Nor, in the end, can idolaters free themselves from the sudden catastrophe that overtakes them (Isaiah 47:11–14). They long ceased to deal with spiritual realities (Isaiah 57:11–13). Their behavior when all was well conditioned their behavior in the time of crisis (Isaiah 45:16, 20). They weren't prepared for the reward of becoming unprofitable servants of God (Isaiah 42:17–25).

Not much imagination is needed to see parallels of ancient image worship in the modern Gentile culture. One of the biggest signs of our times has been a virulent rebirth of images. Although images may not necessarily be evil in themselves, people's partiality toward them and their negative effect on behavior have become causes for concern. The greater part of today's entertainment comes to us in the form of images via television, movies, and videos. They are images of people, of birds, and of beasts, images in color, of male and female.

The graven and molten apparatuses that transmit these images we put up in our own houses as well as in houses set apart for that purpose. Upon these images we dote, preoccupied for hours at a time with our substitute Urim and Thummim. For the images to entertain us, we must bend ourselves down toward them. Preferably, we worship in the dark, heedless of one another. When a social need arises, we resent its intrusion. Our behavior toward one another is colored by what our images dictate. Their power, somehow, is to deflect our entire attention.

Moreover, to acquire an apparatus that transmits these images, we must spend precious resources, laboring for "what is not bread" (Isaiah 55:2). We set our hearts on the privilege of possessing such an apparatus as a worthy goal. In that objective, too, there exists an element of competition with, and thus alienation from, others in our society. Those who invest more resources than our neighbor will enjoy bigger and better images. Of course, we justify this investment on the basis of personal enjoyment. When we invite others to view the images with us, it reinforces us to know that they share the same interests. It normalizes an abnormal pastime.

Recent studies, for example, amply document the unnatural effects of watching television. The images our eyes see are stored permanently in our minds. There they mingle with images of the real world, confusing our perception of reality and affecting behavior. Watching television accustoms people to the sensational, the artificial, the novel, so that they begin to require a regular diet of these things to maintain their interest. This requirement is filled by watching more television or movies, until its addictive effect on people captivates them. Because their minds and hearts dull toward normal everyday happenings, reality seems drab and uninteresting. Television's advertising in part compensate for this dullness by creating unnatural wants or needs in people, which they satisfy by indulging in consumer goods.

More than that, much of television and movies teaches a false social code, enculturating people, especially children, into norms of divorce, disrupted family life, the supremacy of the peer group, affluence, sex stereotypes, alcohol consumption, fast food or junk food habits, coercive health practices, and so forth. Closely linked to this chaotic social structure is this media's false morality. Because so much of television and movies defines no clear-cut standard of right and wrong, it portrays immorality as acceptable. Because the finer human emotions aren't portrayed well in this medium, it inculcates a societal taste for what is depraved, coarse, and unintelligent. It not only vulgarizes the use of language but stunts its development, discouraging reading and intellectual growth.

It should be apparent that the effects of television, movies, and video games, to name but a few instances of modern imagery, parallel those of ancient image worship, turning people's minds and hearts away from God, alienating them through a diet of permissiveness, carnality, and service to a false moral code. The prophets Isaiah and Micah foretell how images will prevail among God's endtime people. Using the common terms "graven images" and "standing images," Micah predicts how people will worship the works of their hands (Micah 5:13; cf. Isaiah 2:8, 20; 17:8).

Jesus' apostle John saw that the ultimate human image will be that of the Antichrist, a tyrannical endtime world ruler. John predicts that all except a very few people will worship his image, an image that "speaks" and commands worship (Revelation 13:4, 14–15). God will bring disaster on those who comply with such worship, however (Revelation 14:9–11; 16:2). Only persons who, on pain of death, resist worshiping the Antichrist's image will merit salvation (Revelation 15:2; 20:4). Of course, for people to pay homage to the Antichrist, those who currently worship images won't need to switch to anything really new. His worship will merely consummate a drama that even now is in full play.

4

VIOLENCE AND SEX

On too many occasions to mention, God warned the Israelites through his prophets of their carelessness in letting their neighbors' Baalism influence them (Deuteronomy 4:1–4; Judges 2:11–13; 8:33). Baalism itself, however, we have not well understood. The cult centers on a mythical account of a life-and-death struggle between the gods. In that story, the hero god Baal overpowers several rivals. He then celebrates his prowess by having intercourse with Anath, his female partner.

The fullest available account of the myth comes from the Baal–Anath Epic of Ugaritic literature. Its alternating scenes of violence and sex, explicit in their descriptive detail, were reenacted in real-life dramas that took their cue from the Baal myth. Pornographic imagery, carved or painted, accompanied such reenactments. The myth so incited the Israelites who exposed themselves to the Baal cult that forthwith they "played the harlot" with non-Israelite women, losing all awareness of their chosen status (Numbers 25:1, 6).

In the Ugaritic account, Baal obtains permission from a higher authority—El (God)—to command the gods Yamm (Sea) and Mot (Death) to comply with Baal's rule or face him in a confrontation. Yamm and Mot represent forces of chaos or disorder that will make trouble for Baal and for the world if Baal doesn't subdue them. They, however, resist Baal's authority and each fights him to the death.

Sundry emissaries and cohorts assist Baal and his rivals in their life-and-death struggle. The versatile craftsman Koshar fashions the weapons Baal uses against his enemies. These weapons can kill, injure, or maim from a distance. As the central figure of the drama, Baal literally kicks up a storm, he being the "Lord" (ba'al) of lightning and thunder. Baal nonetheless suffers reverses and at one time appears dead. But with the timely aid of his violent consort Anath he escapes the clutches of death and wins the victory at the last. The myth thus credits Baal with restoring order in the world, everyone profiting from his extraordinary prowess. Sexual relations between him and Anath, hitherto hampered by adversity, now receive full expression.

In comparing the Baal myth with stories in today's culture, we easily recognize the basic plot that inspires so many movies and dramas of our media. Their very success lies in the amount of violence and sex they display. The hero and his cohorts get authorization to kill and do anything they please, so long as they subdue the enemy and restore order. They do battle using weapons that kill and injure from a distance, weapons that strike swiftly like lightning, that clap aloud like thunder.

In fulfilling his bizarre task, the hero nonetheless experiences setbacks, receives the wounds of battle, and stares death in the face. But help always arrives in the nick of time, often by a woman driven to violence. In these stories, sexual aberrations abound, as they do in the Baal myth. Their scenes of sex and violence appear both subtle and explicit, as they do in the Baal myth. The many variations of their crude stories match their ancient counterparts. In the biblical narrative we thus find Baal-Peor, Baal-Berith, Baal-Zebub, and other Baals.

The spilling over of violence and sex from fictitious dramas into real life is as well attested today as it was among the Canaanites. By making carnality legitimate in their culture, the Canaanites—and later the Israelites who conquered them—marked themselves ripe for destruction. Through the media that constitute an everyday part of our lives, we let characters enter our homes and minds to perform acts we would abhor in real life.

The pornographic images our media depict—the licentious manner of the characters, their distorted standard of values, their predisposition to murder and violence—all subvert and pollute our minds and hearts. Once there, they become a part of us. By indulging such images, we do the contrary of "stopping our ears at the mention of murder, shutting our eyes at the sight of wickedness" (Isaiah 33:15). Yet that standard, an uncompromising standard, God makes a prerequisite of salvation.

5

Pop Music

God has commanded not just ancient Israel but every covenant people to keep themselves unspotted from the world (cf. James 1:27). That commandment applied as much in the days before the Flood as it has since. One account of the period leading up to the Flood appears in an ancient manuscript called the Books of Adam and Eve. They tell how the people of God's covenant, who lived on a high mountain plateau, lost their chosen status when they let the people of Cain entice them down to the plain below, where they lived.

From the days of Adam, God had commanded the people of the covenant "not to mingle with the people of Cain, and not to learn their ways" (2 Adam and Eve 19:4). In the days of Jared—whose name means "going down"—the people of the covenant nonetheless mingled with the people of Cain and soon became as they were. When the Flood came, it swept away both the people of Cain and of the covenant alike. Only Noah and his immediate family, as a type of things to come, preserved their covenant status and were spared (Genesis 6:17–18).

Whether the account the Books of Adam and Eve give is accurate or represents but a folk memory doesn't matter a great deal. What matters are the events it describes, a phenomenon that could occur among any people of God

The Bible predicts that the Flood and the apostasy that preceded it represent something that will be repeated at the end of the world (Matthew 24:37–39; Luke 17:26–27; 2 Peter 3:3–14).

The wickedness and corruption that filled the earth before the Flood, therefore (Genesis 6:5, 12), should forewarn us. We can't presume to be on the side of Noah if we are living the law of the people of Cain. Those whom God preserved through the Flood anciently not only abstained from wickedness but actively resisted its influence (2 Peter 2:5; Jasher 5:22–24).

When, at the Flood, God baptized the earth with water, Noah and his family alone merited deliverance. Similarly, when God baptizes the earth in a flood of fire, only those who are purified "as with fire" will be delivered (Zechariah 13:9; Malachi 3:2; 4:1; 1 Peter 1:7; 4:12–13).

The Books of Adam and Eve identify drunkenness, licentiousness, hatred, murder, and conspiracies as prevalent among the people of Cain (2 Adam and Eve 20:4–10). Scriptural accounts of the period before the Flood concur with that description (Genesis 6:11–13). The prophecies tell us that those same evils will precipitate God's endtime judgments (2 Timothy 3:1–6)—until "the elements melt with fervent heat" (cf. 2 Peter 3:12).

When describing the period before the Flood, the Books of Adam and Eve attempt to spell out what the sacred scriptures say in brief. What most enticed God's people to come down from the Holy Mount and mingle with the people of Cain was the appeal of a certain kind of music. That music possessed the power to ravish people's souls (2 Adam and Eve 20:3). Once the people descended the mountain, all manner of lusts overcame them. The music had conditioned them for that result (2 Adam and Eve 20:20, 30–32).

The music transformed the children of God who had kept his law, who had regularly prayed and fasted, into children of the Devil (2 Adam and Eve 20:15–16, 27, 35). The music robbed people of their self-control and thus of a measure of their agency (2 Adam and Eve 20:3, 9). The music's intensity and momentum, when played at all hours by impassioned musicians, inflamed people's hearts and won them over (2 Adam and Eve 20:2, 4, 12–

13). A godly way of life yielded to the abominations that were the commonplace of the Cainites (2 Adam and Eve 20:34).

The account in the Books of Adam and Eve relates how a man called Genun, whom Satan inspired, made various kinds of trumpets, horns, stringed instruments, cymbals, psalteries, lyres, harps, and flutes and "gathered companies upon companies to play on them" (2 Adam and Eve 20:2, 4). When Genun and his companions played the instruments, "Satan came into them, so that [out of] them were heard beautiful and sweet sounds that ravished the heart" (2 Adam and Eve 20:3). When the bands played, the people of Cain "burned as with fire" among themselves, and as a consequence Satan "increased lust among them" (2 Adam and Eve 20:4).

The bands gathered daily at the foot of the Holy Mount for the purpose of letting God's covenant people hear it (2 Adam and Eve 20:11). After a year of exposure to the music, many of the covenant people went regularly to look down at the musicians (2 Adam and Eve 20:12). Satan then again entered Genun. He "taught him to make dyeing-stuffs for garments of divers patterns, and made him to understand how to dye crimson and purple" (2 Adam and Eve 20:13). To those of the covenant people who came to be entertained, the Cainites "shone in beauty and gorgeous apparel, gathered at the foot of the mountain in splendor, with horns and gorgeous dresses" (2 Adam and Eve 20:14).

When Satan showed Genun a way down from the Holy Mount, Jared admonished the people that if they went down, God would not allow them to return (2 Adam and Eve 20:26). Over a period of time, however, company after company descended until but few remained (2 Adam and Eve 20:30; 21:1). For "when they looked at the daughters of Cain, at their beautiful figures, at their hands and feet dyed in color, tattooed in ornaments on their faces, the fire of sin kindled in them" (2 Adam and Eve 20:31). Moreover, "Satan made them look most beautiful," so that the people lusted after each other like ravenous beasts, committing abominations and falling into defilement (2 Adam and Eve 20:32–34).

When, in remorse, some tried to return up the mountain, they were unable. Having "come down from glory," they had forsaken their purity and innocence (2 Adam and Eve 20:33–34). Through their transgression, to which the music had incited them, the covenant people estranged themselves from being the people of God (2 Adam and Eve 21:4–5).

What strikes us about this story is how it resembles our society today. If we think of the physical descent from the Holy Mount as symbolizing a spiritual descent, the account reads like a contemporary phenomenon. Today, as anciently, the younger generation of God's people has yielded to the enticement of an immoral music.

If you harbor doubts about pop music ravishing the soul, inflaming the heart, or setting passions on fire, just witness a concert by any well-known rock group. The spectacle they create—its fantasy, frenzy, and hysteria—appeals to the very basest of human emotions. The physical appearance of the musicians—their gaudy and glittering attire and their lewd and suggestive gestures—parallel in every way the Cainites whom the Books of Adam and Eve describe. As Isaiah foresaw, "the look on their faces betrays them: they flaunt their sin like Sodom; they cannot hide it" (Isaiah 3:9).

Few would deny that much of pop music today exemplifies what is carnal, sensual, and devilish. Its primitive beginnings, and its maturing into hard, punk, and porno rock, mark it as "the way of Cain," as a "corruption" and a "riot" (cf. 2 Peter 2:12–13; Jude 1:11). Its developing into a modern cult, with its attendant rituals of liquor, drugs, prostitution, and pedophilia, attests to its satanic nature. In many instances, the musicians themselves confess to pacts with Satan, admitting that he inspires their music and lyrics. Scott Temple, a former drug user and a reformed fan of hard rock, called the spirit of the music the "unholy ghost."

Studies show that even milder kinds of pop music are but stepping-stones to hard rock. Attempts to use this worldly medium to convey the celestial message of the gospel is surely an abomination. Syncretism has ever sought to prostitute what is holy and sanction what is profane.

Since pop music and other media have entered Western culture, moral decline in Christian nations has reached an unprecedented low. As in the Babylon of Daniel and his companions, when we hear the sound of horns, flutes, harps, sackbuts, psalteries, dulcimers, and all kinds of music, we worship at the shrine of its creators (Daniel 3:3–15). If any of us, therefore, like Shadrach, Meshach, and Abednego, would walk through the fire in the day of burning (Daniel 3:25; cf. Isaiah 43:2; Malachi 4:1–3), it will be because, like them, we refuse to yield to an idolatrous music.

6

ORGANIZED SPORTS

A second diversion the Cainites used to entice the people of God's covenant, though mentioned only briefly in the Books of Adam and Eve, was organized sports (2 Adam and Eve 20:14). A better-known example of organized sports, which swayed God's people in another age, was the popular Greco-Roman games (cf. 1 Maccabees 1:14; 1 Corinthians 9:24–25). In the Intertestamental and New Testament periods, the single greatest cultural seduction of God's people was Hellenism.

Those who immersed themselves in Greek and Roman culture, including the games, were therefore called Hellenizers or Hellenists. Among Jews, these were principally the Sadducees, an aristocratic priestly class, although Hellenism affected all Jews to some extent. Among Christians from the second century onward, most of the Church's members were Hellenists.

In Palestine, the only legitimate repudiators of Hellenism, either Jewish or Christian, were the Dead Sea sectaries. By leaving their urban brethren and dwelling apart, they formed an early type of the "church in the wilderness." Among the Christians, however, all ended in apostasy, with Hellenism as the chief cause. Both Hellenizers and Jewish sectaries play important roles as historical types, providing a pattern of the endtime.

The Greco-Roman games appear to have originated in religious ritual associated with the ancient Near Eastern fertility cult. An idolatrous amusement—one that turns people's hearts from the law of God to the law of the brute—organized sports had their heyday among the Romans. Although the early Romans adopted many aspects of Greek culture, including gymnasia, athletics, and rigorous disciplining, the Roman appetite, far more than the Greek, tended toward the sensational, the spectacular and barbaric. Many historians connect the decline of Roman civilization to the inordinate disposition the general populace displayed for brute sports.

Participants executed such sports with all the finesse and sophistication civilization could bring to bear. Elaborate stadiums, housing as many as two hundred thousand spectators, with gladiators disciplined and groomed for contests of skill combined with raw strength, characterized sports Roman style. The distinction between the Greek and Roman games coincided, in the main, with the amateur or professional status of the players. While the Greek games were more subdued, nonprofessional events, the Romans went all out in expenditure, professional training, and fanfare.

The games, professional or nonprofessional, included chariot races, track, discus and spear, boxing, wrestling, swordsmanship, and hunting. Men practiced in special barracks or athletic compounds, using different kinds of weight training and exercise. Sports events followed set schedules on the yearly calendar, advertised by posters in every inhabited region. Contests took place in the gymnasia, amphitheaters, and circuses that were common in every city. All classes of society, drawn from cities and neighboring towns, attended the games.

Stadiums typically contained multiple entrances, stairways, tiers, and blocks of seating. Admission was by tickets purchased in advance, or, as in the case of officials, by virtue of reserved seats. Spectators not seated in the immediate proximity of a contest used a primitive form of field glasses. Great bands of musicians, organized in festal processions, blared on trumpets before and at intervals during the games.

Individual contestants often grew very popular. They became household names, whom people knew by their personal statistics and professional records. Women adored gladiators almost as gods. People made predictions on the outcome of the games, betting with one another on the results. Vast, unruly crowds frequented the contests, waving handkerchiefs, shouting advice, approval, and insults, rising up from their seats during moments of suspense. When contests neared their conclusion, the fervor of the crowds often reached fever pitch, accompanied by calls for blood. People debated the results of the games long after the event.

As the decline of Roman civilization set in, the games became the preoccupation of the elite as well as the masses. They devoted exorbitant resources to the games, so much that charitable programs rated a poor second. Of all peoples in the Roman Empire, it seems only pious Jews shunned the games, considering them a heathen pastime.

In our culture today, a widespread preoccupation with sports—football, basketball, baseball, gymnastics, boxing, wrestling, car racing, horse racing, hunting, etc.—must surely make us question whether we, too, like the Romans and Hellenists, are in a state of moral and civil decline. Although our laws prohibit bloodshed, so striking are the parallels that we can't say we are much different. The abandon and frenzy of the human spirit at such events, the foul language, anger, and even bloodlust are reminiscent of the coarse disposition displayed by the Romans.

So all-consuming have today's games become that they govern many people's thoughts, moods, and actions. In the cause of sports, people desecrate the Sabbath. Family life suffers to the point that we hear of "sports widows and orphans." The "next game" becomes more important than our personal victories in working out our salvation.

The fanfare and pageantry we impose on the games, the vast resources of money and hours we devote to organized sports, betray an entrenched cult, a full-blown diversion from life's real contest. In an eternal perspective, it is of no consequence to us whether so-and-so wins a match or whether such and such a team retains its ranking. When we love sports with all our might, mind, and strength, as much of society does, we can only be considered idolaters. Once we catch the infectious spirit of glamorized sports, it won't leave us alone. We must ever be following the progress of a team, making that, not God's "Good News" or gospel, our daily talk, the focus of our thoughts. To be a "fan" or "faithful" of something other than God means we have bought into a substitute of true worship.

This type from the past tells us that organized sports, in their modern, embellished form, are predominantly idolatrous in nature, diverting the mind and heart from being preeminently involved with things of the Spirit. Where sports become an end in themselves, where they evolve into an all-consuming quest for preeminence for its own sake—or for the sake of money or becoming popular with the world, beating the world at its own game—then we overstep the bounds on the side of idolatry.

7

HUMAN IDOLS

The idea of human idols flows naturally out of other forms of idolatry. Indeed, many ancient gods of myth and ritual had human beginnings, some claiming divine parentage or ancestry. Israel's prophets refer to various persons as false gods. Jeremiah calls an apostate ruler in Judah "a despised broken idol" (Jeremiah 22:28). God punishes him by leaving him childless (Jeremiah 22:30)—the covenant curse of having no posterity. Zechariah describes false prophets as idols who speak folly, and he singles out a certain "idol shepherd" who forsakes the flock (Zechariah 10:2; 11:17). Instead of feeding the flock, this religious leader consumes the flesh of the fattest (Zechariah 11:16). God punishes him by smiting him in the arm and blinding him in one eye (Zechariah 11:17) in mock imitation of a marred statue. This punishment renders him ritually blemished and his ministry illegitimate.

Using a subtle play on words, Isaiah identifies prominent figures in society as "idols." By using terms that contain several levels of meaning, he implies that the people idolize certain "celebrities" or "bigwigs"; the people are "enchanted" and "captivated" by them and exhibit "covetous desires," "fawning adulation," and "carnal lust" toward them (Isaiah 1:29–30). The idols, on the other hand, exercise "immunity" from the law on account of wealth, power, or fame; they and their enterprises make up the very spark that sets off a fiery conflagration among the wicked of God's people (Isaiah 1:29–31).

As does the apostle John, Israel's prophets predict that the ultimate human idol is the endtime Antichrist (Daniel 7:19–25; 11:36; 1 John 2:18; Revelation 13:1–8). Biblical types of this arch-tyrant abound: the king of Babylon, the king of Assyria, the king of Tyre, and the king of Greece (Isaiah 10:5–15; 14:4–20; 37:21–29; Ezekiel 28:2–19; Daniel 8:23–25; Habakkuk 2:2–10). To this list we may add later antichrist types, from Nero to Hitler and others. As in the book of Isaiah, the endtime Antichrist is a composite of all evil world rulers who precede him. Like them, he commands people to worship him (Revelation 13:4, 8). Satan lends him his power (Revelation 13:2).

Like a character out of *Star Wars*, the Antichrist rises in the heavens like the morning star to set his throne above the stars of God (Isaiah 14:13). He ascends above the altitude of the clouds and makes himself "like the Most High [God]" (Isaiah 14:14). He sets his nest on high, in order to escape calamities on the earth (Habakkuk 2:9). He exalts himself above all gods, defying even the God of Gods (Daniel 11:36).

With divine irony, God doesn't let the Antichrist arise until the world is full of false gods. Worshiping this human idol is but an extension of what is already rampant. As God's instrument, the Antichrist condemns to the fire the false gods of all peoples, including the idols of God's people (Isaiah 10:10–11; 37:18–19). He regards no god other than himself but "magnifies himself above all" (Daniel 11:37).

Under his tyrannical rule, all human idols now worshiped, exalted, extolled, glorified, revered, idolized, and adored will be things of the past. Pop stars, movie stars, sports stars, superstars, tycoons, barons, and bigwigs will be but "despised broken idols." Through the instrumentality of the Antichrist, God will "make all glorying in excellence a profanity and the world's celebrities an utter execration" (Isaiah 23:9). Until Jesus displaces the Antichrist as King of Kings and Lord of Lords when he comes in glory, the Antichrist's coercive worship will serve as retribution for our present voluntary worship of man.

8

IMAGINATIONS OF THE HEART

Virtually every instance of the expression "imaginations of the heart" in the Bible equates such imaginations with idolatry and following other gods. At a covenant ceremony, Moses warns Israel, "Lest there should be among you a man, woman, family, or tribe whose heart turns away this day from Jehovah our God to go and serve the gods of these nations; lest there should be among you a root that bears gall and wormwood" (Deuteronomy 29:18).

Moses cites a classic kind of self-deception, at the same time harking back to the curses he has just enumerated in connection with God's covenant: "And it come to pass, when he hears the words of this curse that he blesses himself in his heart, saying, I shall have peace [salvation], though I walk in the imagination of my heart to add drunkenness to thirst" (Deuteronomy 29:19).

Moses thereby gives us to understand that self-deception, or "drunkenness," follows a personal lack or "thirst" for the knowledge of God. Paul restates that interpretation, saying that imaginations, or reasonings and rationalizations, are a kind of conceit or pretense that exalts itself "against the knowledge of God" (2 Corinthians 10:5). Moses concludes his warning by showing how God won't withhold his anger and jealousy from those who indulge vain imaginations but will bring "all the curses written in this book" upon them, separating them for evil from his people, blotting out their name from under heaven (Deuteronomy 29:20–21).

Fantasies or "imaginations of the heart" are nonetheless something each of us has to live with. They are an integral part of being mortal, expressing a person's innate disposition to contemplate both good and evil. Unavoidably, however, "the imagination of man's heart is evil from his youth" (Genesis 8:21) in the sense that both good and evil present themselves to him. People retain a natural tendency to be proud, mischievous, and wicked (Proverbs 6:18; Luke 1:51).

But when they let the imaginations of their heart rule them, when they don't "make captive every thought in obedience to Christ" (2 Corinthians 10:5), then they fall. Then, though "they knew God, they glorified him not as God, neither were thankful, but became vain in their imaginations, and their foolish heart was darkened" (Romans 1:21).

When called on to repent, they think, "There is no hope," and they continue following their own devices, relying for guidance on the imaginations of their heart (Jeremiah 18:12). Instead of heeding God's counsel, they listen to those who say, "You will have peace; . . . no evil shall befall you" (Jeremiah 23:17). In the end, God esteems them as good for nothing and vents his wrath upon them (Jeremiah 13:10–14). Biblical types of falling prey to the imaginations of the heart include the people before the Flood, the people at the Tower of Babel, and the kingdoms of Israel and Judah before their exile (Genesis 6:5; 11:6; Isaiah 39:5–7; Jeremiah 11:7–10).

Without identifying everything today that would qualify as fantasies or "imaginations of the heart," it seems evident that what is worldly and subject to change—all things "new," novel, fashionable, or in vogue; all trends, fads, crazes, and gimmicks; in short, all that is not of God but concocted in the minds of men—God dooms to destruction along with those who love those things. They make up but a passing parade of phantoms intruding upon our senses, whose purpose is to confuse and to befuddle. Because imaginations of the heart vary constantly, those who follow them know no stability. Every wind of change, as it were, sweeps them away.

God, and what is of God, doesn't behave so. In God, there exists no relativism or variableness. Unlike man, he doesn't walk in crooked paths or turn to the right or to the left, nor does he vary from what he has said. His thoughts don't reflect our thoughts, nor his ways our ways (Isaiah 55:8). As the heavens are higher than the earth, so are his ways higher than our ways and his thoughts higher than our thoughts (Isaiah 55:9).

An important aspect of imaginations of the heart is evident in the way we think. Patterns of negative thinking that prevail today may prevent us from discovering the truth about ourselves and thus from realizing our divine potential. Satan, the "father of lies," would have us believe that we don't qualify for the promises God holds out to us, or that we *do* qualify for his promises though we don't keep God's commandments. We hear these attitudes expressed in statements such as "I would rather die in the nuclear blast" or "I am not to blame for my mistakes." By engaging in self-deception, basing our actions on false premises, we sell ourselves short of divine blessings. We endanger our lives as we face perilous times and deny the good effect of God's love.

9
NATURE CULTS

The prophet Isaiah refers to nature worship that is prevalent among God's people. Nature worship deviates from true worship in that it seeks out a substitute for Paradise. To Isaiah, a preoccupation with parks or gardens (*gan*; *gannâ*) spells idolatry (Isaiah 1:29–30).

He speaks of those who "choose" or "cherish" the nature experience in the act of forsaking their God (Isaiah 1:28–29). These nature worshipers provoke God to his face by "sacrificing in parks, making smoke upon bricks" (Isaiah 65:3). Their favorite resorts include canyons, ravines, and riverbeds (Isaiah 57:5–6). They spend nights in hideaways, among green trees and under the crags of cliffs and rocks (Isaiah 57:5–6; 65:4). There, they burn with lust and commit fornication with one another (Isaiah 57:5; 66:17). They eat the flesh of animals prohibited in the Mosaic Code (Isaiah 65:4; 66:17). They pour drink libations as a toast to their cult and consume polluted beverages (Isaiah 57:6; 65:4).

Those not of their lifestyle they bid keep their distance, considering themselves "holier than thou" (Isaiah 65:5). They amuse themselves over God's true worshipers, though they themselves are the slaves of sin (Isaiah 5:18; 57:4). Heedless, and in abrogation of their own agency, they imitate the behavior of people who are popular (Isaiah 66:17). Called the "offspring of adulterer and harlot," they are born of sin, "a spurious breed" (Isaiah 57:3–4), the product of an apostate people beset by satanic influences. The nadiral act of their wickedness is molesting and sacrificing children to their god (Isaiah 57:5). In a similar manner, God makes an end of them in the day of his burning wrath (Isaiah 66:17, 24).

Different kinds of nature worship in our modern culture repeat the ancient pattern. Of course, outdoor recreation isn't in itself idolatrous. Many families go on an annual campout, which may be a happy bonding experience. Others people like hiking in the mountains as a means of communicating with God. Such experiences have little to do with idolatry.

But there exist many aberrations of the nature experience that *are* idolatrous. From overemphasizing perfection in home gardens and landscaping while disregarding the needy who pass by in the street, to showing an inordinate passion for outdoor gatherings, with near ritualistic preparations of carefully selected foods, the same self-gratifying imbalance seems to mark the society of God's people then and now. Isaiah could have had the current camper culture in mind when he observed idolaters "hitched to transgression like a trailer" (Isaiah 5:18).

Those among us for whom nature has become a religion seem to outdo even the primitive cult. The fervid weekenders in their sport, and even backyard enthusiasts, display a sophistication the ancients could not have guessed. Today's proliferation of campers, dirt bikes, dune buggies, four-wheelers, skis, snowmobiles, yachts, speedboats, gliders, and related accoutrements betoken a rampant and costly cult. That cost, moreover, more often than not includes breaking the Sabbath.

Many nature worshipers escape responsibility toward God and humanity by frequenting pristine places. The beauties of nature can excite the romantic instinct in people, while nature's seclusion can pave the way for licentiousness and sexual deviance. Nature religionists do virtually as they please away from the common constraints of society. The emergence of satanic cults today, with their bizarre outdoor and indoor rituals, attests to the corruption of our society after the manner of the Israelites of old. When recreation becomes an end in itself, when promiscuity seeks out recreation as a means of self-expression, that is idolatry.

10

MAMMON OF UNRIGHTEOUSNESS

God's Word in all ages warns humanity what Jesus expresses so well, that the "mammon of unrighteousness" (Luke 16:9)—the riches of this world—have been and will be the downfall of countless souls; that we cannot serve God *and* mammon. Each is a master to be loved at the expense of hating the other (Matthew 6:24; Luke 16:13). So numerous are scriptural counsels warning about the riches of this world that we must suppose they dulled the ears of those who perished with their riches. Or perhaps the rich didn't think of themselves as rich and so didn't apply these warnings to themselves.

From the way sacred scriptures emphasize equality among God's people (cf. 2 Corinthians 8:12–15), we see that God's idea of the rich draws a contrast between the haves and have-nots. In that sense, being rich means possessing a surfeit when others lack. Such inequality alienates people from one another.

God's Word delineates the dominant characteristics of the rich. Persons, for example, who "hasten to be rich have an evil eye" and aren't innocent (Proverbs 28:20, 22). They soon fall into temptations and snares, into foolish and hurtful lusts, which "drown men in destruction and perdition" (1 Timothy 6:9). Trusting in "uncertain riches" (1 Timothy 6:17), people grow wise in their own conceit (Proverbs 28:11) and wax proud. They lift up their hearts because of their riches (Ezekiel 28:5), refusing to give heed to the Word of God and becoming unfruitful (Matthew 13:22).

The rich pass over the deeds of the wicked and don't judge the needy's cause (Jeremiah 5:28). They despise the poor and drag them before the judgment seats (James 2:6). They set their hearts on riches and the vain things of the world, scorning and persecuting those who don't believe according to their will and pleasure (cf. Micah 6:12). The rich defraud and condemn the just, supposing they are better than them. In brief, the love of money is the root of every kind of evil, causing people to "err from the faith" (1 Timothy 6:10).

When their treasure is their god, the rich suffer evil consequences. The rich can hardly enter the kingdom of heaven because they already have their consolation (Matthew 19:23; Luke 6:24; 16:19–25). They lay up treasures for themselves on earth, only to lose their souls (Luke 12:16–21). They carry nothing of their glory or riches beyond the grave (Psalm 49:16–17).

In the day of burning heat, the rich fade away like withering grass whose flower falls (James 1:11). The riches they have swallowed down, they must vomit up again (Job 20:15). Riches "profit not in the day of wrath" (Proverbs 11:4). The rich who don't give of their substance to the poor will lament in God's Day of Judgment, crying, "The harvest is past, the summer is ended, and we are not saved" (Jeremiah 8:20; cf. Revelation 18:1–19). In the great day of God's judgment, the rich hide themselves in dens, crying to the mountains and rocks, "Fall on us, and hide us from the face of him who sits on the throne, and from the wrath of the Lamb" (Revelation 6:15–17).

If men don't learn how to administer the unrighteous mammon, how can God commit to their trust the true riches? (Luke 16:11). As for the rich, they "do good" if they are ready to distribute their wealth to those in need and are willing to communicate with them (1 Timothy 6:18). God justified the wealthy Zacchaeus, a hated publican who climbed a tree in order to greet him (Luke 19:2–9). Zacchaeus regularly gave "the half of my goods . . . to the poor; and if I have taken anything from any man by false accusation, I restore [to] him fourfold" (Luke 19:8).

We can justify pursuing riches, therefore, but only within a narrow compass—for the intent to do good—to clothe the naked, feed the hungry, liberate the captive, and administer relief to the sick and the afflicted. Those charitable purposes are the sole scriptural justification for pursuing riches.

The people of the Church at Laodicea had grown rich and increased in goods, lacking nothing (Revelation 3:17). Spiritually, however, they were wretched, miserable, poor, blind, and naked (*ibid.*). Because they were neither hot nor cold but lukewarm toward the gospel, God spewed them out of his mouth (Revelation 3:16). Hosea describes Ephraim as saying, "I have become rich, I have found me out substance. In all my labours they shall find no iniquity in me" (Hosea 12:8). But God responds that he will yet make Ephraim dwell in tents (Hosea 12:9).

11

CULTURE OF BABYLON

The name Babylon means many things to many people. The Hebrew word (*babel*) goes back to a kingdom Nimrod founded, where the ancients built the great tower of Babel, or Babylon (Genesis 10:9–10; 11:1–9). That kingdom evolved into an idolatrous materialistic civilization that reached its zenith in the powerful Neo-Babylonian empire of Nebuchadnezzar (cf. Daniel 2:37–38). The prophet Isaiah identifies Babylon typologically as both a people and a place: the sinners and the wicked, the earth and the world (Isaiah 13:1, 9, 11). He predicts that endtime Babylon will suffer the fate of Sodom and Gomorrah, thus likening the world's desolation to a fiery cataclysm falling upon the wicked (Isaiah 13:4–19).

Jeremiah calls Babylon a "destroying mountain" (*har hammashît*), an expression that in Hebrew also means a "corrupting" or "decadent" kingdom (Jeremiah 51:25). Babylon's destiny is to become a burned mountain, desolate forever, because Babylon corrupts and thus ultimately destroys all the earth (Jeremiah 51:25–26). Babylon's endtime fall is a key event that ushers in the earth's millennial age of glory (cf. Revelation 17:1–19:8; Isaiah 21:9).

Isaiah and Jeremiah single out a feature of Babylon that corrupts people, namely the manufacture, promotion, and sale of idols—the works of men's hands. Those who engage in it become "Babylon" themselves and in the end perish with it. A story told of how Abraham's father, Terah, in the land of Ur of the Babylonians, at times put young Abram in charge of his store. When Terah, who made and sold idols, went into the forest to fetch wood for their manufacture, Abraham was to sell the idols in his father's place. Abraham would nonetheless dissuade buyers, reproving the adults for esteeming mere statues as gods.

One day, fed up with his duty, Abraham smashed all his father's wares except a large idol that stood on the top shelf. When Terah returned from the forest, he flew into a rage, demanding an explanation. Abraham responded caustically, "The big one did it!" implying that these were no gods or they could have saved themselves. After that, Abraham became unpopular in Ur and the people sought his life.

The essence of this sort of idol worship is not that people really believed the idols to be gods but that their manufacture, promotion, and sale provided them with a living. It became a socio-economic system that afforded urban dwellers a means of sustenance. One problem with that system lay in its false economic base and the instability it bred—it fed on itself.

Economic factors determined social behavior—the law of supply. Manufacturing the works of men's hands yielded income but constituted idolatry, because what so many people worked at, oriented their lives to, was ultimately unproductive. The work of idols didn't sustain itself but demanded to be sustained. It enslaved to a false idea not merely those directly involved with it but also those who produced foodstuffs and raw materials because the latter were required to labor additionally in order to provide for the rest.

The reverse of this phenomenon also applied: false spiritual values influenced directions the economy would take—the law of demand. Because of their association with deity, idols represented something socially acceptable into which people might pour time and money. The prestige the idols furnished made people protective of the system. Those who prospered from it had found a niche. Their *real* source of subsistence—farming and husbandry—took second place. People measured wealth in terms of money and the idols money could buy rather than in terms of how much food or commodities could be produced.

We can thus liken Babylon's socio-economic structure to an upside-down pyramid, which, as it grows, ever narrows at its base. In it, the many depend on the few for their support. Babylon's mass of people, engaged in producing and selling idols, remain out of touch with their life source, rendering them vulnerable to catastrophe. The greatest height to which Babylon attains is thus also its lowest point of stability. For when, through some unforeseen divine intervention, a single stone jars from its base, the entire structure collapses.

By way of contrast, on the other hand, Zion's economy is not so structured. As Israel's prophets depict, Zion possess a broad rural base in which every family works its inheritance of land. That structure makes Zion stable and self-sustaining. In it, abide neither poor nor those who appropriate what belongs to others. Zion's people look to their Head, their cornerstone, to bless them with increase.

Old Testament examples show that such a structure can weather most storms, endure most attacks, and quickly repair or rebuild itself. Direct means of sustenance—the capacity to produce foodstuffs and raw materials—is ready at hand. Even when people must flee temporarily into the wilderness, their link to the land provides them with the greatest maneuverability.

In short, the works of men's hands on which people set their hearts, on which they spend natural and human resources, are by definition "idols" (Isaiah 2:8; Jeremiah 10:1–5). As the prophets describe them, they are idols that people invent, design, sketch, carve, forge, molten, cast, weld, plate, fit, hammer, rivet, and mass produce (Isaiah 40:19–20; 41:7; 44:10, 12–13; 45:16; Jeremiah 51:17). Manufactured, promoted, and sold for gold and silver (Isaiah 44:9; 46:6), the idols are the fruits of a technology of well-nigh magical proportions (Isaiah 47:10, 12). They follow trends and engage the whole of society (Isaiah 44:11; 47:13). Depending on what kinds of idols, people both carry them about and set them in place in their homes (Isaiah 45:20; 46:7).

The entire production of idols, however, is erroneous and vain (Jeremiah 51:17–18). It causes people to become like the idols themselves, sightless and mindless to things spiritual, unaware and insensible to impending disaster (Isaiah 42:17–20; 44:9, 18; 45:16). It constitutes a "wine" that makes people drunk and mad—the wine of Babylon (Jeremiah 51:7; cf. Revelation 18:3).

As a law unto itself, Babylon tyrannizes and enslaves, yet people don't discern it for what it is (Isaiah 44:20; 47:6–8, 10). In reality, Babylon suffers from gross defects, open wounds no one can heal (Jeremiah 51:8–9). At its height, it mounts up to heaven, from whence God suddenly and utterly casts it down (Jeremiah 51:8, 53–58). On its destruction, those who are intoxicated with its wine don't even wake up from their sleep (Jeremiah 51:39, 57). Because their gods—the works of men's hands—didn't save them, they profited them nothing in the end (Isaiah 44:9–10; 46:7).

Although at Judah's exile Jeremiah advised his people to serve the king of Babylon (Jeremiah 27:6–17; 40:9), Jeremiah didn't mean, When in Babylon, do as Babylon does. Indeed, Isaiah and Jeremiah looked forward to the time Israel would leave Babylon before God destroyed it (Isaiah 48:20; Jeremiah 51:6). The time would come, as with Abraham, when it would no longer be advisable to remain in Babylon. The more it ripened in wickedness, the less possible it would be to live *in* Babylon but not *be* of Babylon.

Isaiah depicts God's people's coming out of Babylon in a new exodus patterned after Israel's ancient exodus out of Egypt (Isaiah 48:20–21; 52:11–12). He compares the gathering of a repentant remnant of Israel from the ends of the earth to Abraham's coming out of Babylonia into the wilderness (Isaiah 41:8–9; 51:1–3). The prophets, therefore, speak both of a spontaneous exodus from Babylon on the eve of its destruction and of a gradual, premeditated exit before that time (cf. Isaiah 57:1). As the example of Lot's wife illustrates, those ensconced in Babylon find it hard to leave at a moment's notice.

Doing "the works of Abraham"—in order to merit a glory that compares to his (cf. John 8:39)—thus includes leaving Babylon as he did, becoming wholly pure of its abominable idols (cf. Isaiah 51:2; 52:11). Not unexpectedly, the limits of any alternative to Babylon are narrow. In Hebrew prophetic thought, what is not Zion is Babylon and what is not Babylon is Zion.

In effect, there exist only two choices for God's people: either build up Zion or build up Babylon. That decision requires that we gain a clear idea of what Zion and Babylon are—how the prophets define them, what they stand for, and how to implement Zion. Isaiah, for example, defines Zion as both a people and a place: Zion is those of God's people who repent and also the place to which they gather, a safe place in God's Day of Judgment (Isaiah 1:27; 4:5–6; 35:10; 59:20). According to Isaiah, God's people must urgently repent of Babylonian idolatry, of worshiping the works of men's hands (Isaiah 2:5–8; 17:7–8; 46:3–9).

Scriptural precedents prove the principle that those who leave Babylon under God's direction inherit a Promised Land as did Abraham and his company (Genesis 12:1–7). According to Jeremiah, a person leaves Babylon in order to go to Zion, throwing in one's lot with God by an everlasting covenant (Jeremiah 50:1–5). To leave Babylon means to go out from among the wicked to establish Zion somewhere else. All who remain in Babylon do so at the peril of their lives (cf. Isaiah 48:17–19; Jeremiah 51:6).

As for the works of men's hands in today's Babylon, little more need be said to recapture the ancient scene. Essentially the same materialistic economy that prevailed then prevails in our day. Like the ancient port city of Tyre, Babylon's mercantile arm (cf. Isaiah 23; Ezekiel 26–28), endtime Babylon encompasses every kind of trade and merchandise—whatever the people's souls lust after by way of material possessions (Revelation 18:1–24). The manufacture and promotion of contemporary works of men's hands comprise a virtually unlimited enterprise. Reduplicating the socioeconomic structure of ancient Babylon is the very stuff of modernization.

Technology of almost magical dimensions consumes us to the point of enslaving us to it. By orienting our entire lives around their production, sale, and maintenance, we set material things above our relationship with God. Our focus on caring for the works of men's hands and servicing them is synonymous with loving and serving idols. And yet, as with its ancient counterpart, we don't discern modern Babylon for what it is. The wine with which all nations of the earth are drunk blinds us to Babylon's looming collapse (Revelation 17:1–2; 18:2–3). As with many other peoples who have grown up in captivity, we ourselves don't recognize, or else take for granted, the fact of our bondage.

12

THE ARM OF FLESH

To Israel's prophets, Pharaoh king of Egypt epitomizes the arm of flesh on which God's people lean in times of national crisis. Ancient Egypt—a type of the world's great endtime superpower—exemplifies human industry, wealth, and political stability (Ezekiel 31:2–9, 18). In God's Day of Judgment, however, Pharaoh proves to be but "a splintered reed that enters and pierces the hand of any man who leans on it" (Isaiah 36:6; Ezekiel 29:6–7). When put to the test, Egypt's ample resources of chariots and horsemen prove no match for the ruthless world power from the North God raises up against his people (Isaiah 19:4; 20:4; Jeremiah 43:10–12; 46:1–26; Ezekiel 29:19–32:32).

By making treaties and alliances with foreign nations, God's people only add sin to sin, rejecting God's covenant and instead relying on the arm of flesh (Isaiah 30:1–2). The very act of God's people turning to human strength for protection causes their hearts to turn away from their true source of strength (Jeremiah 17:5–8). In response, God denies his protection and shames his people, causing them and their allies to fall before their enemies (Isaiah 30:3–5; 31:2–3; Ezekiel 17:16–21; 30:1–8). Although God prepares a way of escape for the righteous of his people, by far the majority don't "see when good comes" because they eyes are turned in the wrong direction (Jeremiah 17:6).

But the arm of flesh assumes forms other than relying on men's armies and weaponry. All constitute idolatry because they put humanity before deity. They overlook God as the Author and

Creator of all, as he who holds all things in being. God gives life and takes it away, often in ways that seem miraculous or untimely. God himself raises up adversaries, individual and national; and God disposes of them (Exodus 22:23–24; 1 Kings 11:14, 23; Isaiah 10:5–17; 54:16–17).

Even as God promises his people a land of inheritance and an enduring posterity—as a covenant blessing, on condition they live righteously—so he promises to protect them in the face of mortal threats. Israel's prophets don't predict that God will destroy the righteous in his Day of Judgment. On the contrary, he grants salvation both temporal and spiritual to those who keep his commandments. In the theology of Israel's prophets, temporal and spiritual salvation go hand in hand (Isaiah 8:9–15; 55:3; Jeremiah 21:8–9; 27:12–17; Ezekiel 18:1–32; 33:1–20; Amos 5:1–15).

Perhaps some of God's people may die in order to fill up the measure of their sacrifice or as a testimony against the wicked (Isaiah 51:17–23; Jeremiah 51:49; Ezekiel 9:5–7; Daniel 11:33–35; Revelation 6:9–11). Nevertheless, personal righteousness, in the endtime as anciently, is the only criterion for being delivered from death (Isaiah 33:14–16; Jeremiah 51:45; Ezekiel 9:4, 6; Daniel 7:26–27; Revelation 9:4).

Isaiah, therefore, reduces every kind of dependence on things human to a "Covenant with Death" (Isaiah 28:15, 18). That covenant includes looking back on past victories and glories (Isaiah 28:1, 4), believing human predictions of a bright future for humanity (Isaiah 30:10; 47:13), relying on the outward observance of worship (Isaiah 29:1, 13), being guided by anything less than divine revelation (Isaiah 28:7–13), contriving secret schemes and contingency plans (Isaiah 28:15; 29:15; 30:16), plotting machinations and intrigues (Isaiah 30:12; 47:12), and every other way of "taking refuge in deception and hiding behind falsehoods" (Isaiah 28:15).

In God's Day of Judgment, people's Covenant with Death proves void. A terrible scourge overruns those who trust in the arm of flesh (Isaiah 28:18). All means of warding off woe by somehow indemnifying against it will then disastrously default (Isaiah

47:11–15). These will prove to be merely bonds that bind people down to destruction (Isaiah 28:22).

At the last, human agreements and alliances will be held in contempt and come to nought (Isaiah 8:9–15; 33:7–8; 47:13–15). The compacts people make are deceitful—no brother can be trusted (Jeremiah 9:4–6). Even as they speak together in peaceable terms, people lie in wait to take advantage of one another (Jeremiah 9:8). In short, all who trust in human counsel are under a curse and will be broken.

It is no secret that manmade pacts pervade Western nations today. At the national level, leaders set up such compacts as the UN, NATO, SEATO, and so forth, ostensibly for the welfare and protection of all. Leaders nonetheless regard simultaneous arms buildups as essential for self-preservation. Conversely, treaties governing disarmament make nations vulnerable to betrayal, as happened before World War II.

At the individual level, we may trust in securities, bonds, indemnities, or similar provisions without focusing on the source of all good. Relying on human helps to fortify against future disasters betrays a lack of trust in God who governs all affairs. Sometimes these helps substitute for the welfare and protection that come from keeping covenant with God alone. By seeking such "benefits," people may feel relieved of personal accountability. Being primarily concerned for their physical wellbeing, their spiritual welfare suffers.

Another consequence of trusting in man is that, once made, human contracts can be undone often only with dishonor and loss of face. In God's eyes, we can't simply walk away from our word (Ezekiel 17:15–21). Biblical examples, however, show that the worst feature of human agreements is the mindset people develop. The disposition of those who rely on the arm of flesh holds them in its grip like a disease.

Although people might acknowledge God, they can't bring themselves to believe there exists any other way. Like all idolatry, relying on the arm of flesh blinds people to a higher purpose and providence—that God saves those who trust in him (Isaiah 42:17–43:4). Such an alternative is an intangible that scares people to death (Isaiah 51:12–13). Even when God brings upon them all kinds of extremities, many remain insensible to the cause (Isaiah 42:22–25). They can't relate current woes to their own actions. Although they exercise good intentions after suffering God's chastisements, they remain as prone as ever to trust in man before trusting in God (Jeremiah 42:1–44:30).

But when they exercise faith in the divine source of all good (Jeremiah 33:3, 9), when they cease to put man's counsel before God's (Isaiah 29:15), when they stop playing God by killing those who should live and keeping alive those who should die (Ezekiel 13:19), when they truly make God their Judge, Lawgiver, and King (Isaiah 33:22), then God extends his promise to them. In the end-time destruction he has decreed upon the world, some he will endow with power from on high as a testimony against those who depend on human strength (cf. Daniel 7:27; Revelation 14:1–3). In that day, a remnant of Ephraim will find him a sure source of strength to repulse the attack at the gates (Isaiah 28:5–6).

13

Elitism–Pharisaism

Elitism–Pharisaism simultaneously partakes of social pride and hypocrisy. It is idolatry because it puts the institution or peer group before the person—the individual serves the collective, not vice versa. It is worship of the system or organization to which people belong and is therefore a kind of self-worship. Typifying that sort of idolatry are the Pharisees of New Testament times, a group whose elitist tendencies we know well from Jesus' discourses with them.

Pharisaic persons display a form of godliness that lacks the power thereof (2 Timothy 3:5). They harbor a presumptuousness about being a chosen and elect people (Luke 3:8). They consider their humble brethren a lost and fallen people, to be despised as lesser mortals (John 7:47–52).

A paradoxical aspect of the elitist-pharisaic phenomenon is that its pastors and teachers could, in fact, possess authority to teach and instruct (Matthew 23:1–3). In reality, however, they have taken away the key of knowledge and shut up the kingdom, neither entering it themselves nor letting others enter (Matthew 23:13; Luke 11:52).

As a result, they can't answer difficult religious questions nor recognize the signs of the times (Matthew 16:2–3; 22:46). They are blind leaders of the blind, yet they assume they see things aright (Matthew 15:14; John 9:41). They confuse their priorities and what is real (Matthew 23:16–24; Luke 11:42). They cancel the good effect of God's Word in people's lives by overriding individual devotion with manmade conventions (Matthew 15:3; Mark 7:13).

Yet, observant in their religion and highly esteemed by men, these mediators of God's Word regard themselves as righteous by their own standards (Luke 16:15; 18:11–12). But their religion consists only of what appears in public (Matthew 23:5). Their private thoughts and conversations tell another story (Luke 12:1–3). Outwardly, they appear righteous, but inwardly they raven like wolves, yielding to wickedness, oppression, and excesses (Matthew 23:25–28; Luke 11:39). Although they believe in Messiah, they care more for people's praise than for God's (John 5:44; 12:42–43). Like leaven in bread, hypocrisy permeates their establishment (Luke 12:1).

Their hypocrisy, likewise, inspires their communal prayers (Matthew 23:14). They love for others to call them by their ecclesiastical titles, to greet them publicly and hold them in admiration (Matthew 23:7; Luke 11:43). In token of reserved seats in the kingdom of heaven, they take the foremost seat in meetinghouses and at banquets (Matthew 23:6; Luke 14:7–8). Yet they quickly find fault with persons who don't conform to their exterior of worship (Mark 2:18, 24; 7:2, 5; Luke 6:7).

While they themselves covet the things of the world, they despise those who mingle with sinners in attempts to rescue them (Matthew 9:11; Luke 7:33–34; 16:14). Their fear of political repercussions outweighs their love of spiritual obligation (John 11:47–48). In the end, they disfellowship those who love and confess Messiah (John 9:22; 12:42). The converts to their form of religion, whom they go to great lengths to gain, they make twofold more children of hell than themselves (Matthew 23:15). So much hypocrisy governs their lives that it appears incurable (Matthew 23:29–33).

To assure themselves that their religion is well founded, the elitist-pharisaic faction makes frequent mention of a key prophet or forebear on whom they base their authority (Matthew 3:9; 19:7; Luke 20:28; John 9:28–29). So far have they departed from the prophet's message, however, that if some came among them who taught as he did, they would seek to kill them as did their forefathers (Matthew 23:30–34; Luke 11:47–49).

Were their acclaimed prophet to confront them, however, he would be the first to assert that neither God's love nor his Word abides in them (John 5:38, 42, 45). Thus, the most righteous among them—one like their acclaimed prophet—they call a deceiver and make a scapegoat (Matthew 27:63; John 11:50). At that point, God removes the kingdom from them, giving it to a people who will bring forth its fruit (Matthew 21:43).

In summing up this somber biblical type, we see among the ancient elitist Pharisees many forms of priestcraft that Jesus and his apostles predicted would corrupt his endtime church. Indeed, the things they prophesied that would befall his people repeat the pharisaic phenomenon as nearly as any scriptural type.

Just as the ancient Pharisees' love had waxed cold because of iniquity among them, so will the love of God's endtime people wax cold because of iniquity (Matthew 24:12). As they loved themselves and were covetous and treacherous, so will they be (2 Timothy 3:1–4). As they were ever learning but never coming to a knowledge of the truth, so will they do likewise (2 Timothy 3:7). As they admired men for personal advantage, so will they (Jude 16). As they failed to believe that enemies would invade and destroy their land, so will they be willingly ignorant of their role in precipitating God's fiery destruction upon the wicked (2 Peter 3:3–10).

As a consequence, just as messianic imposters from among the Jews preceded Jesus' first coming (Acts 5:36–37)—with the notable exception of John the Baptist—so false christs and prophets will precede his second coming (Matthew 24:5, 11, 23–24; Mark 13:6, 21–22). The true prophets they will nonetheless withstand, just as the false prophets withstood Moses (2 Timothy 3:8–9) and as the Pharisees withstood Jesus (Matthew 26:62–68; Luke 20:1–2; John 8:48).

The righteous among them, they will hate and betray (Matthew 24:9–10; Mark 13:12–13), just as the Jews hated and betrayed Jesus and his disciples to the ecclesiastical and political authorities of the day (Matthew 26:47–27:26; Acts 6:11–15; 18:12–17). Many they will deliver to councils to be judged and punished for their testimonies of the truth, smiting some and killing them unlawfully (Matthew 24:9, 49; Mark 13:9), even as they delivered Jesus and his disciples to be persecuted and killed by their enemies (Luke 22:47–23:24; Acts 7:57–59; 12:1–4).

In God's Day of Judgment that will then be upon them, they will suffer the fate of all hypocrites. Cutting them off from his people, God will cast them into outer darkness, where there is weeping and gnashing of teeth (Matthew 8:12; 13:41–42; 24:48–51; 25:29–30).

14

POLLUTION OF THE TEMPLE

A kind of idolatry that caused God's presence to depart from his people as invading armies advanced upon them (Ezekiel 8:6; 9:1–11) was pollution of the temple. Several forms of such idolatry polluted the house of God anciently, including a "symbol of envy," a manmade idol at its entrance (Ezekiel 8:3, 5), people viewing images portrayed on a wall (Ezekiel 8:10–12), Israel's elders making clouds of incense or sweet odors (Ezekiel 8:11), women bewailing the death of a popular cult figure (Ezekiel 8:14), and men worshiping the great luminary (Ezekiel 8:16).

Because God's people polluted the house of God by setting up their abominations in it (Jeremiah 7:30; 23:11), the temple proved no place of protection in the time of God's judgment (Jeremiah 7:4–10). When enemies invaded the land, they destroyed the temple (Jeremiah 52:13) or polluted it yet further by setting up their own abominations in it (1 Maccabees 1:54). Beginning at the temple, they slew all except a certain few whom God protected (Ezekiel 9:6–7). The latter sighed and wept continually because of the abominations in their midst (Ezekiel 9:4).

The pollution of churches and meetinghouses today with manmade objects and external stimuli creates distractions from the Spirit of God that might otherwise prevail, repeating the ancient type. People's hearts' and minds' preoccupation with their idols turns religious services into a façade of worship. Are not the ancient mourners who sighed and cried for the wickedness of the people a type of endtime souls whose lives God preserves while the rest worship him in vain? Where, today, are the few who weep for the sins and abominations in their midst?

CONCLUSION

Considering that these and many additional types of idolatry dominate the modern world, should we expect any result other than what happened to God's people in the past? Aren't the nations who inherited Israel's spiritual blessings—who, in spite of serious lapses, maintained their belief in the Judeo-Christian God—now facing a general slide into the same malaise that infected Israel of old? Won't the climate of political correctness that justifies every aberration from norms of behavior God laid down for his ancient people not lead to the same unthinkable fate today? In view of the fact that believers in God now inhabit the entire earth, if those judgments of God were to come upon us today would that not spell the end of the world as we know it?